DOGS
ARE GREAT BUT

WRITTEN BY ŠTĚPÁNKA SEKANINOVÁ / ILLUSTRATED BY ADAM WOLF

THEY SAY THAT DOG IS MAN'S BEST FRIEND.

THEY'LL NEVER LET YOU DOWN, THEY'RE DEVOTED TO YOU, AND THEY'RE LOTS OF FUN . . .

A LIFE WITHOUT A DOG IS A SAD ONE. WHO ELSE CAN YOU HANG OUT WITH WHEN ALL YOUR FRIENDS ARE GONE? WHO ELSE CAN YOU TELL YOUR DEEPEST SECRETS TO?? UNFORTUNATELY, THOUGH, SOME PARENTS DON'T THINK IT'S THE BEST IDEA TO GIVE THEIR KID A FOUR-LEGGED FRIEND, AND THEY DON'T TRUST THEM TO TAKE CARE OF THEM PROPERLY.

SO WHAT DO WE DO?

WE PROVE WE CAN DO IT!

SEE WHAT I'M DOING? I'M WALKING A DOG. YOU CAN'T SEE HIM, THOUGH, CAN YOU? OF COURSE YOU CAN'T! BECAUSE I'M WALKING MY IMAGINARY DOG. RAIN OR SHINE, I TAKE HIM OUT FOR HALF AN HOUR EVERY MORNING, BRIGHT AND EARLY AT 6:00 A.M., EVEN ON THE WEEKEND. SOON, I WILL CONVINCE MOM AND DAD THAT I'M SERIOUS ABOUT GETTING A DOG.

IT'S GREAT TO HAVE A DOG, BUT . . .

MY PARENTS SAID "GOOD JOB!" FOR ALL MY HARD WORK. AS OF TODAY, I'M HAPPY TO SAY THAT I'M THE PROUD OWNER OF A REAL LIVE PET DOG.

IT'S AWESOME WHEN DREAMS COME TRUE! I NOW HAVE A REAL, HONEST-TO-GOODNESS DOG AT HOME, AND THINGS ARE SO MUCH MORE FUN. NO MORE PRETEND DOG FOR ME! MY REAL DOG BARKS, WHINES, LICKS MY FACE, AND WAGS HIS TAIL WHEN HE'S HAPPY.

Heeeeeyyy Buddy?!
Come on, let's play!

WITH YOUR NEW FRIEND CLOSE AT YOUR HEELS WHEREVER YOU GO, BOREDOM IS A THING OF THE PAST.

ALTHOUGH THINGS ARE NOWHERE CLOSE TO TIDY ANYMORE, ALL THE FUN AND EXCITEMENT MAKES IT TOTALLY WORTH IT . . .

IT'S GREAT TO HAVE A DOG, BUT . . .

DOGS PEE AND POO WHEREVER THEY WANT.

DON'T MOVE! YOU'RE ABOUT TO STEP IN THAT PUDDLE ON THE FLOOR.

TO KEEP OUR FURRY FRIEND FROM POOPING AND PEEING ON THE LIVING-ROOM CARPET, WE'VE GOT TO TEACH THEM DOGGY HYGIENE. AFTER EVERY MEAL, DRINK, AND NAP, WE HAVE TO TAKE THEM OUTSIDE. SOON, THEY'LL GET USED TO DOING THEIR BUSINESS OUTSIDE!

JUST LIKE HUMAN BABIES NEED DIAPERS, SPECIAL PADS ARE MADE FOR DOGS, CALLED TRAINING PADS. ALWAYS PUT THE PAD IN A SPECIAL SPOT IN YOUR HOUSE — BY THE DOOR IS BEST — AND YOUR PUP WILL LEARN WHERE TO DO THEIR BUSINESS.

THERE WILL COME A TIME WHEN YOUR DOG NO LONGER NEEDS THE TRAINING PAD AND WILL PREFER TO PEE AND POO OUTSIDE.

IT'S GREAT TO HAVE A DOG, BUT . . .

OUR DOG TEARS AND CHEWS EVERYTHING IN SIGHT.

ALL OUR SLIPPERS ARE GONE. OUR SHOES ARE READY FOR THE TRASH BIN. AND THAT'S NOT COUNTING OUR NEW SOFA . . .

OH NO! OUR DOG CHEWED UP MY SISTER'S FAVORITE DOLL. SHE CRIED ALL DAY LONG.

WHAT DO WE DO? IF OUR DOG KEEPS CHEWING EVERYTHING UP, MY SISTER WON'T BE TOO HAPPY ABOUT IT.

IF IT'S RAINING OUTSIDE,
A LONG WALK IS OUT OF
THE QUESTION. BUT THERE'S
FUN TO BE HAD AT HOME TOO.

YOUR DOG — JUST LIKE YOU — NEEDS TO USE THEIR BRAINPOWER.
COME UP WITH FUN ACTIVITIES THAT'LL GET THEM THINKING.
HIDE A FEW YUMMY TREATS AROUND THE ROOM AND HAVE YOUR
PUP GO FIND THEM. THIS GAME IS SURE TO GET THEM EXCITED!
TO KEEP THIS GAME FRESH, MAKE THE HIDING SPOTS HARDER
AND HARDER TO FIND.

WHEN YOU'RE DONE WITH THE BRAIN
GAMES AND THE WEATHER IS GOOD
AGAIN, GO OUTSIDE TO PLAY FRISBEE
WITH YOUR POOCH.

GIVE YOUR PUP LOTS OF
ACTIVITIES AND YOU'LL NEVER
HAVE TO WORRY ABOUT THEIR
TEETH CAUSING TROUBLE.
NEVER SAY NEVER – BUT
YOU GET THE IDEA!

CALMER BREEDS:
IF YOUR DOG ISN'T RUINING
YOUR FURNITURE, THAT'S GREAT!
BUT DON'T TAKE IT FOR GRANTED — MAKE
SURE YOUR PUP NEVER GETS BORED.
GIVE THEM PLENTY OF PLAYTIME AND
ACTIVITIES TO KEEP THEM ENTERTAINED.

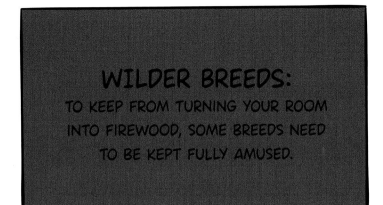

WILDER BREEDS:
TO KEEP FROM TURNING YOUR ROOM
INTO FIREWOOD, SOME BREEDS NEED
TO BE KEPT FULLY AMUSED.

IT'S GREAT TO HAVE A DOG, BUT . . .

THEY'RE DRAGGING ME OUT OF BED TOO EARLY!

ARE YOU AN EARLY BIRD — SOMEONE WHO LOVES GETTING UP EARLY? WELL, TOO MUCH OF A GOOD THING CAN BE A BAD THING. IT'S NOT EVEN LIGHT OUTSIDE YET, AND ALREADY YOUR DOG IS TUGGING AT YOUR BLANKET, ASKING TO BE LET OUT . . . AND THEIR WISH IS YOUR COMMAND.

GOING OUT!

TAKING CARE OF A PET CAN TAKE YOU OUTSIDE OF YOUR COMFORT ZONE. IT MIGHT BE HARD, BUT YOU'LL BE REWARDED WITH A THANKFUL, CHEERFUL, AND — MOST IMPORTANTLY — LOVING PUP. IT'S TOTALLY WORTH IT!

GUARD DOG

DO THE EMPTY STREETS OF THE EARLY MORNING AND
EVENING MAKE YOU NERVOUS? DO YOU SENSE DANGER
LURKING AROUND EVERY CORNER? DON'T WORRY —
YOU HAVE YOUR FAITHFUL DOG BUDDY BY YOUR SIDE!
THEY'LL NEVER LEAVE YOU BEHIND. IF ANYONE JUMPS
OUT AT YOU, YOUR PUP WILL HAVE YOUR BACK!

TEACHING YOUR DOG
TO WALK ON A LEASH:

HOLD THE LEASH IN ONE HAND, SOMETIMES USING YOUR OTHER HAND TO HOLD IT STEADY.

A SLACK LEASH IS BETTER THAN A TIGHT ONE. WHEN YOUR DOG IS WALKING NICELY, KEEP PRAISING THEM.

DON'T PRAISE THEM WHEN THEY BITE THE LEASH, THOUGH!

AND DON'T PRAISE THEM WHEN THEY PULL ON THE LEASH, OR TRY TO CHANGE YOUR DIRECTION.

SOMETIMES IT'S FUN TO LET YOUR DOG EXPLORE
ON THEIR OWN BY TAKING OFF THEIR LEASH.
BUT IF A CAT OR ANY OTHER ANIMAL COMES
THEIR WAY, YOUR JOY MIGHT NOT LAST LONG.

AT TIMES, YOU MIGHT ENCOUNTER SOMEONE
YOUR DOG STARTS BARKING AT. BEFORE YOU'RE
READY TO LET YOUR DOG OFF THE LEASH,
YOU HAVE TO TEACH THEM TO RESPOND
TO THE BASIC COMMAND "COME HERE!"

IT'S GREAT TO HAVE A DOG, BUT . . .

WHEN IT'S RAINING OUTSIDE, THEY BRING MUD INDOORS

HOME AT LAST FROM YOUR WALK THROUGH THE DELUGE!

YOUR DOG IS SOPPING WET AND SUPER
MESSY. SHOULD YOU DRY THEM OR PUT
THEM STRAIGHT IN THE BATH? NEITHER
SOUNDS LIKE TOO MUCH FUN, BUT THIS IS
WHAT YOU DO WHEN YOU'RE A DOG OWNER.

WHAT IF YOUR FOUR-LEGGED FRIEND IS
EXTREMELY DIRTY? WELL, ALL YOU CAN DO
IS PUT THEM IN THE BATHTUB OR SHOWER
FOR A GOOD DOG-SHAMPOOING.

IT'S GREAT TO HAVE A DOG, BUT . . .

A DOG IS NOT LIKE A DOLL. NOT ALL OF THEM LOVE HAVING THEIR HAIR COMBED!

ONE DAY, YOUR DOG COMES HOME FROM THEIR WALK LOOKING LIKE A MESS. YOU'VE GOT TO GRAB A COMB AND GIVE THEM A GOOD BRUSHING. IN FACT, LONG-HAIRED DOGS NEED TO BE COMBED OFTEN – AT LEAST ONCE A WEEK!

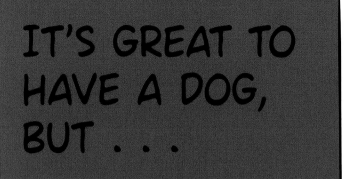

YOUR PUP'S HAIR NEEDS REGULAR CARE, DEPENDING ON ITS TYPE. SOME DOGS HAVE A DOUBLE COAT – A TOP LAYER OF LONG OR SHORT COARSE HAIR, AND A BOTTOM LAYER OF SOFT AND THICK HAIR. SHORT-HAIRED POOCHES NEED A GOOD BRUSHING, WHILE LONG-HAIRED ONES NEED THE TOP HAIR PARTED SO THE BOTTOM HAIR CAN BE BRUSHED.

TYPES OF HAIR

MANAGEABLE COAT: IDEAL FOR THE BEGINNING DOG OWNER; REQUIRES BRUSHING ONLY ONCE A WEEK

SILKY COAT: DEMANDING; CATCHES CONES, THISTLES, AND OTHER BOTHERSOME STUFF.

LONG COAT: PRONE TO TANGLING AND MATTING.

CURLY OR WAVY COAT: DOESN'T SHED, BUT NEEDS REGULAR WASHING AND CUTTING.

HAIRLESS COATS: ONLY THEIR COATED PARTS (TAIL, EARS) NEED BRUSHING; SUNSCREEN NEEDED ON SUNNY DAYS.

COARSE COAT: REQUIRES REGULAR BRUSHING TO REMOVE DEAD HAIR.

IT'S GREAT TO HAVE A DOG, BUT . . .

WHAT ABOUT DOG FASHION?

WHENEVER YOU'RE OUT WALKING, HAVE YOU EVER SEEN A DOG WEARING A COOL JACKET OR STYLISH BOOTIES? IT MIGHT NOT JUST BE BECAUSE THEY'RE FANCY DRESSERS – IT'S ALSO FOR THEIR HEALTH!

DOG WHO LIVE IN A COMFY HOME ALL YEAR – NO MATTER THE WEATHER – AREN'T AS TOUGH AS THEIR DOG COUSINS WHO LIVE OUTSIDE. SOMETIMES, WE NEED TO DRESS OUR FURRY FRIEND IN A COZY SWEATER OR A RAINCOAT TO KEEP THEM WARM AND DRY.

OLDER DOGS LOVE WEARING COZY SWEATERS! SHORT-LEGGED, SMOOTH-HAIRED, AND HAIRLESS BREEDS NEED A COAT IN WINTER, ESPECIALLY IF YOUR WALK IS A LONG ONE!

NO DOG SHOULD HAVE TO SUFFER THROUGH COLD WINTER DAYS! EVEN A LONG-HAIRED POOCH NEEDS PROPER WINTER ATTIRE – SNOW CLINGING TO LEG HAIR IS NO FUN. THE VERY IDEA WOULD MAKE YOU WANT TO STAY INDOORS, WOULDN'T IT?

HOT CONCRETE AND SCORCHING SAND, COLD SNOW AND ICY SIDEWALKS – IT'S ALL TOO TOUGH FOR SENSITIVE PAWS. DOGS NEED SPECIAL SHOES TO PROTECT THEIR PAWS FROM ROUGH TERRAIN AND FREEZING SURFACES . . .

IT'S GREAT TO HAVE A DOG, BUT . . .

SOMETIMES THEY GET SICK.

TO KEEP YOUR DOG FRIEND HEALTHY AND HAPPY, TAKE THEM TO THE VET REGULARLY FOR SHOTS AND "DEWORMING" (REMOVING THEIR WORMS). WORMS ARE YUCKY PARASITES THAT CAN MAKE YOUR PUP SICK . . . SO GET RID OF THEM!

JUST LIKE US, DOGS SOMETIMES GET HURT OR EAT SOMETHING THAT MAKES THEM SICK. BUT DON'T WORRY! A VET CAN HELP THEM FEEL BETTER — FROM SMALL PROBLEMS TO BIG ONES.

AN X-RAY CAN SHOW IF A DOG HAS EATEN SOMETHING IT SHOULDN'T — LIKE A TENNIS BALL. SOMETIMES SURGERY IS NEEDED, AND AFTERWARDS A COLLAR IS PUT ON TO KEEP THE PUP FROM BITING THEIR STITCHES.

EVEN THE STRONGEST DOG CAN BREAK A BONE. AS THEY RECOVER, THEY'LL LOOK LIKE A HALLOWEEN MUMMY!

UPSET TUMMIES ARE ONE OF THE MOST COMMON DOG PROBLEMS. DOGS OFTEN EAT THINGS THAT AREN'T GOOD FOR THEM OR THAT THEY CAN'T DIGEST. IF YOUR PUP HAS AN UPSET TUMMY, YOU NEED TO PUT THEM ON A DIET. A DIET CAN ALSO HELP IF YOUR PUP IS HAVING TROUBLE GOING POTTY, WHICH CAN MAKE THEM REALLY UNCOMFORTABLE.

FOOD THAT DOGS CAN'T EAT

TOMATOES

ORANGES

AVOCADO

GARLIC

SWEETS

GRAPES

CHOCOLATE

ONION

CHERRIES

ALMONDS

BOILED BONES

FOOD SUITABLE FOR DOGS

EGG

HERBS (PARSLEY, BASIL, AND OREGANO ARE GOOD, BUT AVOID NUTMEG, GARLIC, AND ONION POWDER; AND SAGE, ROSEMARY, AND THYME)

COOKED MEAT
(MAKE SURE TO REMOVE ANY BONES)

SPECIAL DOG PELLETS

RAW BONES
(WHILE COOKED BONES ARE DANGEROUS, RAW BONES ARE FUN FOR THEM TO CHEW ON)

FISH
(MAKE SURE IT'S COOKED AND REMOVE ALL THE BONES)

SOME FRUITS
(JUST REMOVE ALL THE SEEDS AND CORES)

RICE

EXTRA VIRGIN

SWEET POTATOES
(JUST MAKE SURE THEY'RE COOKED)

VEGETABLES
(CARROTS, GREEN BEANS, AND BROCCOLI ARE GREAT, BUT AVOID ONIONS, GARLIC, AND WILD MUSHROOMS)

OLIVE OIL
(DON'T GIVE THEM TOO MUCH)

IT'S GREAT TO HAVE A DOG, BUT . . .

WHAT DO WE DO WHEN WE GO ON VACATION?

WHAT IF YOU HAVE TO CHOOSE BETWEEN GOING TO THE MOVIES WITH YOUR FRIENDS OR WALKING YOUR DOG? YOU COULD EITHER MISS OUT ON THE FUN OR GET SOMEONE ELSE – LIKE A BROTHER OR A SISTER – TO TAKE YOUR DOG FOR A STROLL.

BUT WHAT DO YOU DO WITH YOUR DOG WHEN YOU WANT TO GO ON A VACATION WITH YOUR FAMILY?

INSTEAD OF GOING ON VACATION, YOU COULD STAY IN AND WATCH A MOVIE WITH YOUR DOG. BUT THAT'S PROBABLY NOT THE ADVICE YOU WANTED . . .

YOU COULD FIND SOMEONE NICE ENOUGH TO SPEND TWO WEEKS LOOKING AFTER YOUR PET.

YOU COULD BOOK YOUR DOG A STAY AT A DOGGY HOTEL.

HOTEL

THE MOST FUN SOLUTION, THOUGH, IS TO JUST TAKE YOUR FOUR-LEGGED FRIEND ON VACATION WITH YOU!

IT'S GREAT TO HAVE A DOG, BUT . . .

THEY WON'T STOP BARKING AND BARKING!

SOME DOGS COME WITH A CERTAIN FEATURE WE NEED TO REMEMBER — SOMETHING WE CAN EASILY FORGET WHEN PICKING A PET. SOME DOGS REALLY LOVE TO MAKE THEMSELVES HEARD. SO THEY BARK, HOWL, AND WHINE, WHICH CAN BE REALLY ANNOYING FOR OUR NEIGHBORS.

YOU CAN'T DO ANYTHING TO STOP IT – BARKING AND HOWLING IS IN A DOG'S NATURE. YOU JUST HAVE TO HOPE YOUR NEIGHBORS ARE JUST AS UNDERSTANDING AS YOU ARE.

NOW THAT YOU'VE MADE IT TO THE END OF THE BOOK, DO YOU STILL WANT A DOG? YOU DO?! GREAT! CONGRATULATIONS! YOU HAVE PROVEN THAT YOU ARE SERIOUS. BELIEVE US, DESPITE SOME DIFFICULTIES, BEING A DOG OWNER IS WELL WORTH IT. SO GET READY FOR SOME FUN TIMES WITH YOUR FURRY FRIEND!

GLOSSARY OF CANINE COMMUNICATION

DOG BODY LANGUAGE

TAIL-FLICKING	SLOW AND CALM TAIL-WAGGING
Yay, I'm so excited!	I'm perfectly satisfied
TAIL TUCKED BETWEEN THE BACK LEGS	BODY TENSED, TRYING TO LOOK BIGGER
I'm scared	I'm not afraid of you
CROUCHING DOWN	LYING ON THEIR BACK, EXPOSING THEIR BELLY
Your wish is my command	I am completely devoted to you

MOUTH	HEAD AND EYES	EARS
TIGHTENED CORNERS OF THE MOUTH I'm wary!	**HEAD UP, EYES STRAIGHT AHEAD** I'm self-confident	**EARS FLATTENED DOWN ON THE HEAD** Don't scare me! I don't understand you.
CORNERS OF THE MOUTH PULLED DOWN, TEETH BARED Go away! Now!	**EYES FIXED AND SQUINTING** Don't test met or I'll attack	**HEAD TURNED AWAY** I am in a peaceful mood
YAWNING I'm feeling pretty chilled out	**EYES FIXED, MOUTH OPEN** I'm such a happy dog	**HEAD TILTED TO THE SIDE** Hmm. I'm a bit confused

DOGS
ARE GREAT BUT

© B4U PUBLISHING FOR ALBATROS,
AN IMPRINT OF ALBATROS MEDIA GROUP, 2024
5. KVĚTNA 1746/22, PRAGUE 4, CZECH REPUBLIC
AUTHOR: ŠTĚPÁNKA SEKANINOVÁ
ILLUSTRATIONS © ADAM WOLF
TRANSLATOR: ANDREW OAKLAND
EDITOR: SCOTT ALEXANDER JONES

PRINTED IN CHINA BY LEO PAPER GROUP

WWW.ALBATROSBOOKS.COM

albatros